Into the Sea

Into the Sea

Brenda Z. Guiberson
Illustrated by Alix Berenzy

Henry Holt and Company • New York

For the toothless turtle, a survivor of wetlands, woodlands, oceans, and deserts for more than two hundred million years

—B. Z. G.

For Kelly

—A. B.

Henry Holt and Company, Inc., *Publishers since 1866*
115 West 18th Street, New York, New York 10011
Henry Holt is a registered
trademark of Henry Holt and Company, Inc.

Published in Canada by Fitzhenry & Whiteside Ltd.,
195 Allstate Parkway, Markham, Ontario L3R 4T8.

Library of Congress Cataloging-in-Publication Data
Guiberson, Brenda Z.
Into the sea / Brenda Z. Guiberson; illustrated by Alix Berenzy.
Summary: Follows the life of a sea turtle from its hatching on a beach
through its years in the sea, and its return to land where it lays its eggs.
1. Sea turtles—Juvenile literature.   2. Sea turtles—Life cycles—Juvenile literature.
[1. Sea turtles.   2. Turtles.]   I. Berenzy, Alix, ill.   II. Title.
QL666.C536G82   1996   597.92—dc20   95-46757

ISBN 0-8050-2263-5
First Edition—1996
Printed in the United States of America on acid-free paper.∞
1   3   5   7   9   10   8   6   4   2
The artist used a blend of color pencil and gouache on black paper
combined with gouache on white paper to create the illustrations for this book.

*A portion of the proceeds from this book will be donated to the
Caribbean Conservative Corporation / Sea Turtle Survival League, a nonprofit organization
dedicated to the preservation of sea turtles and other marine and coastal wildlife.
Caribbean Conservation Corporation
4424 N.W. 13th Street, Suite A1, Gainesville, FLA 32609.*

Tap, tap. Scritch. The tiny sea turtle is the last hatchling to break out of her leathery egg and crawl up the sides of a sandy nest. She is not much bigger than a bottle cap and would make a good meal for a hungry sea bird or a crab. But at this moment, at dawn, the crabs are resting in muddy burrows and the beach is quiet and empty.

The turtle smells the sand and stares at the bright moonlight that glistens across the ocean. She rests a moment and then, like a windup toy, pulls herself quickly across the beach with her flippers. Always she heads straight for the silvery moonlight. *Clack, click-clack.* A crab pops out of its burrow and sees the dark moving shape. Just in time, the turtle reaches the edge of the water. A gentle wave splashes across her back and carries her into the sea.

Instinctively the turtle knows how to paddle with her flippers and dive beneath the surface. She is still swimming hard when the sun moves into the sky. Every few minutes she comes up for a breath of air. Her eyesight is much better in the water. She sees a jellyfish, a starfish, and a barracuda with a big mouth. None of them see the turtle. Her white underside blends in with the shimmering white surface of the ocean.

Splop. The turtle comes up for air in a patch of sargassum weed. A tiny crab and a water strider ride on the floating raft. Below, a sargassum fish uses the plant for camouflage. They all drift with the winds and current while the weeds hide them from the sharp-eyed sea birds above and the hungry fish below. The little turtle floats around in the clump for several months, eating tiny plants and animals called plankton.

As the turtle grows, her shell grows with her and gets a little harder. She likes to dive into long streams of seaweed that grow on the ocean bottom. There, mussels and seahorses sift water for plankton to eat. When a strong current comes up, the seahorses grab on to the seaweed with their tails, while the mussels hold on to rocks with threadlike feet. But the little turtle is not yet strong enough to swim against this current. She drifts away with the moving water.

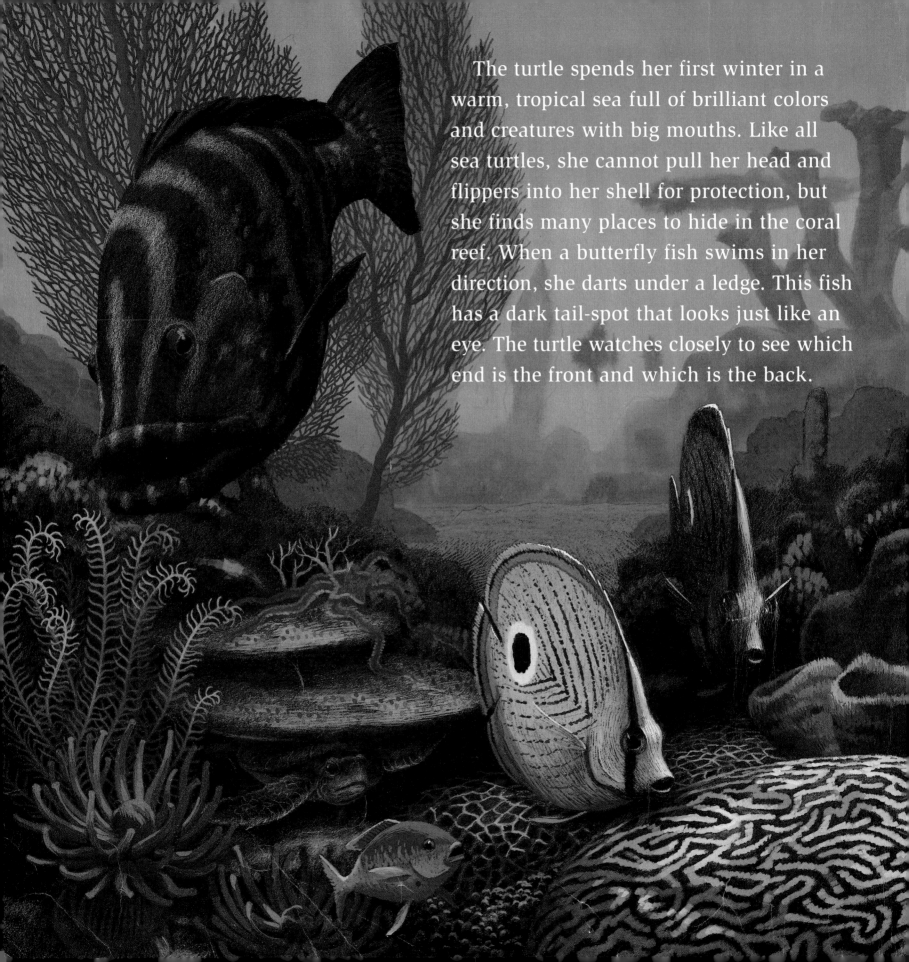

The turtle spends her first winter in a warm, tropical sea full of brilliant colors and creatures with big mouths. Like all sea turtles, she cannot pull her head and flippers into her shell for protection, but she finds many places to hide in the coral reef. When a butterfly fish swims in her direction, she darts under a ledge. This fish has a dark tail-spot that looks just like an eye. The turtle watches closely to see which end is the front and which is the back.

By now the turtle has been in the sea for over a year. She is as big as the sea birds and most of the fish. She has developed strong swimming muscles and swims four times faster than a human.

The turtle has no teeth but bites off pieces of seaweed with the sharp ridges of her jaw. She spends two whole months eating her way through a rich, wavy garden of sea grass.

After several more years, the turtle grows into one of the biggest creatures in the sea. Sharks, however, are still a danger. When one comes near her feeding area, she swims out into a warm current far away from the shallow ocean shelf. She crosses deep, deep water where sunlight cannot reach the bottom and seaweed cannot grow. There is not much to eat in the middle of the ocean, but she continues on her long journey, living on the extra fat in her body.

Even a big turtle can get very tired.
Sometimes she stops to sunbathe on
the surface of the water. The sunlight
discourages the barnacles and marine
grasses from growing on her shell. She
likes to float for hours in the midday
sun. A remora, with a special fin on its
head, attaches to her underside for a
free ride. Then a tired brown booby
flutters down to join them for a rest
on the surface of the ocean.

The turtle hears humpback whales singing in the sea. She dives underwater and the bird flies away. She passes a humpback swimming in slow circles and blowing a ring of thick bubbles. Many small fish get caught in the swirling, whirling water of this bubble net. With a strong push of its fluke, the whale comes up through the middle and swallows hundreds of trapped minnows in one huge gulp. The turtle swims swiftly away, but the remora stays behind to catch a ride on the whale.

At three hundred pounds, the turtle is a fully grown adult. Soon eggs begin to form in her body, and she finds a current that seems familiar to her and follows it back across the ocean.

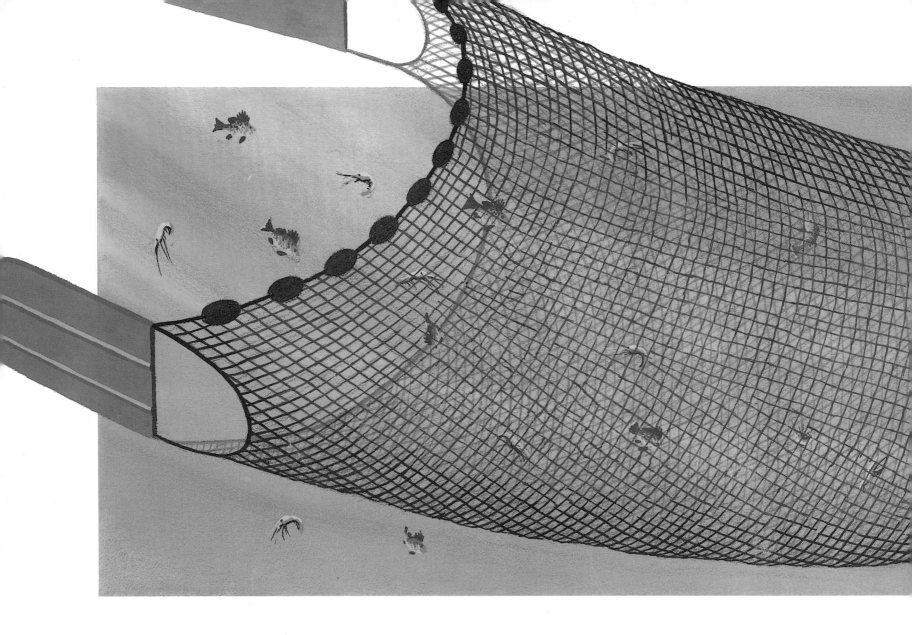

The turtle swims deep under the water for almost two hours, but before she comes up to breathe, she swims below a fishing boat. Suddenly she finds herself trapped in a net. Each time she tries to swim away, her flippers scrape the sides of the net and almost get tangled in the woven ropes.

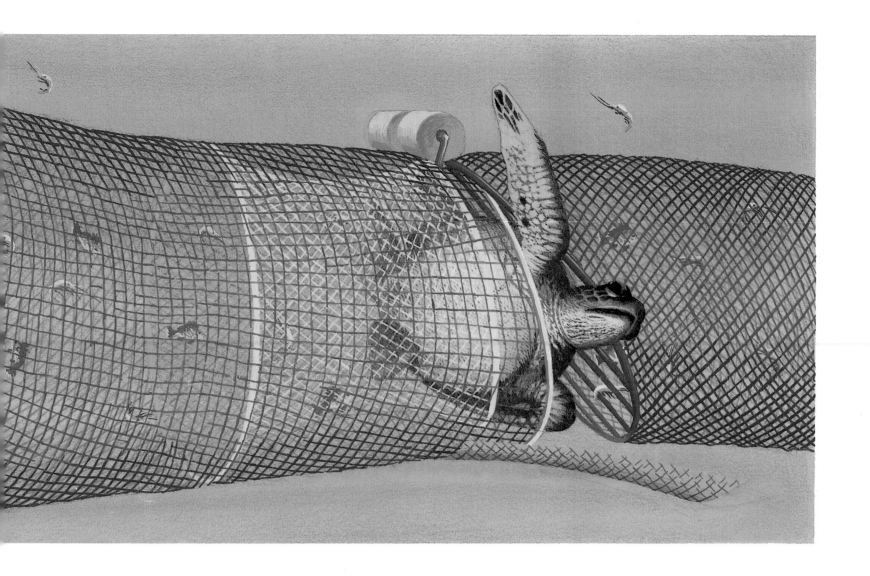

She bumps into metal bars. *Clunk.* Shrimp and small fish swim through the slots between the bars, but the turtle is much too big. She swims over them and finds an escape door at the bottom. Soon she is at the surface of the ocean, taking in big gulps of fresh air.

After a rest, the turtle follows the same familiar current through the sea. She swims many hundreds of miles in this flow of water. Finally she crosses over the top of one ocean mountain and along the steep side of another. When she pops her head out of the water, she sees the top of the second mountain. It is a round island, with a warm sandy beach.

There are many other turtles just like her in the water. Some are male and some are female. A male swims up to her and nuzzles her head. He swims in front of her, touches her flippers, and gently nips her shoulder. They mate and he fertilizes her eggs. The male turtle swims out to the deep ocean, but she swims off in the other direction.

After more than twenty years in the sea, the turtle returns to the land. She waits until nighttime, when the tide is high, to come in. She is slow and awkward as she pulls her huge body up onto the sandy beach. She does not see well on land. Tears stream down her cheeks, as they do in the water, to help her body get rid of extra salt from the sea. She pokes her nose into the sand. The turtle seems to know that she has come back to the same island where she was born.

Slowly she drags herself across the beach. When she gets near a small bush, she stops to rest and then begins to dig a nest in the sand with her flippers. *Thump, scrape, whoosh, wheeze*. It is hard work as she scoops out a hole for her body and a deeper chamber for her eggs. Sand flies everywhere, covering her back and head. She works for three hours, laying over one hundred eggs and then covering them with sand.

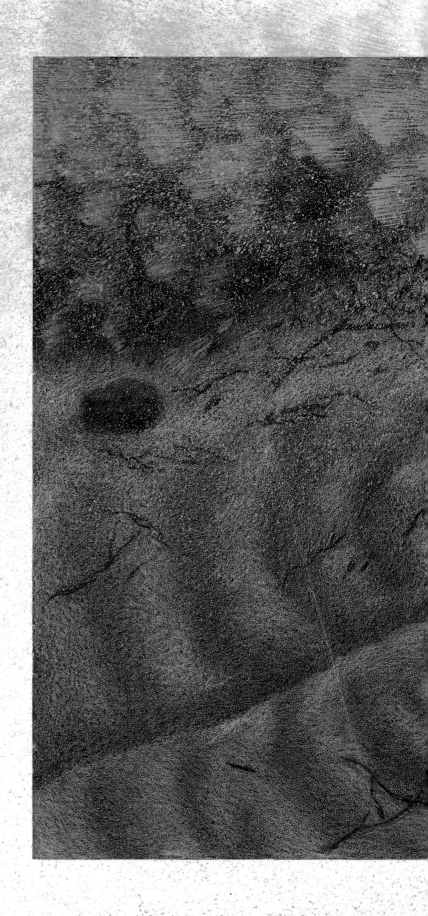

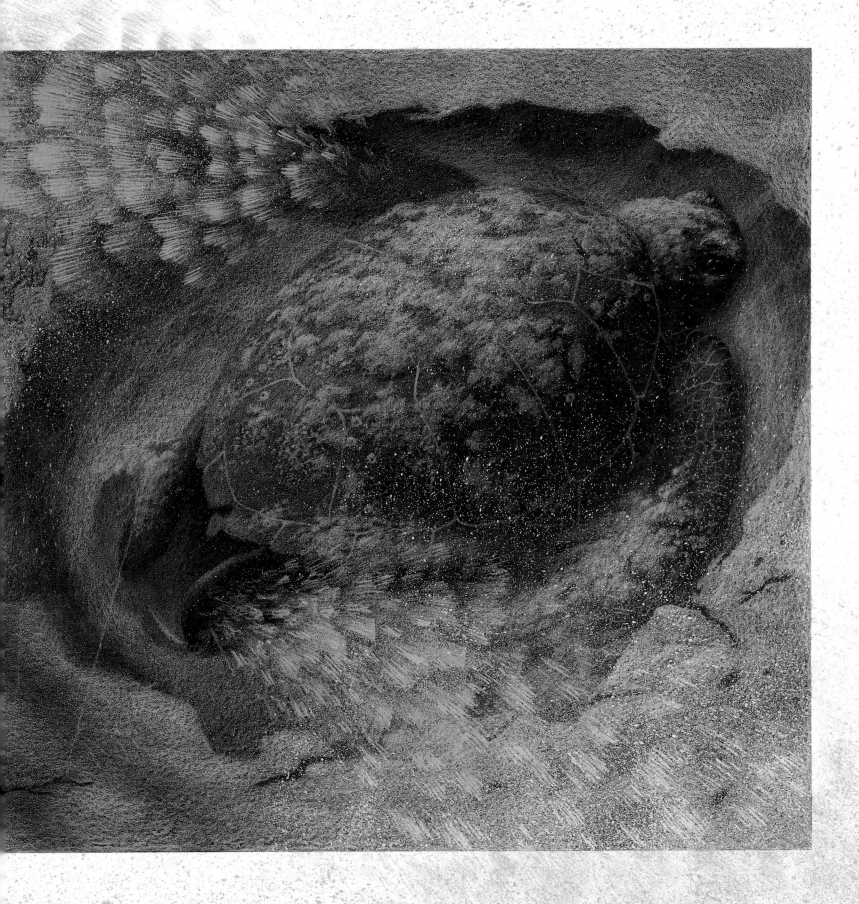

Once again the turtle crosses the beach. Waves sweep the sand off her back and lift her into the water. Her huge body feels lighter and she sees clearly again. She leaves the sandy nest behind her. If nothing destroys the eggs, her babies will hatch in two months. Perhaps one or two will get past the crabs and the sea birds, the fish and the fishing nets, and like their mother, will return to lay eggs on the same sandy beach before making their way back into the sea.

Fast in the Sea, Slow on the Sand

Leatherback
74 inches

Green turtle
49 inches

Loggerhead
47 inches

Flatback
39 inches

Hawksbill
35 inches

Kemp's ridley
30 inches

Olive ridley
30 inches

It is a difficult and delicate venture for a sea turtle to leave the ocean and lay her eggs on land. In the exposed setting of sand and shallow water, things can go wrong for the turtle, her eggs or hatchlings.

Centuries ago, settlers, explorers, and pirates landed on New World beaches and discovered the turtle nesting sites. They ate turtle eggs, grabbed the slow, plodding females as they crossed the sand, and caught turtles that came up for air or basked on top of the ocean. Turtles were flipped on their backs and stacked alive on ship decks until fresh meat was needed by the cook. It didn't take long for the population of sea turtles to decline dramatically.

There are other problems for these reptiles. Some turtle eggs are crushed by vehicles on beaches, while others are eaten by dogs, raccoons, jaguars, and snakes. Hatchlings get caught by birds, crabs, and fish, and larger turtles are killed so that fancy items may be made from their shells. And then there are the many turtles that die in fishing nets or after swallowing plastic or other debris in the ocean.

Today sea turtles and their eggs are protected by law, but they still face the loss of their nesting places. Many resorts, homes, and hotels have been built on nesting beaches. Still, turtles return to these beaches and lay eggs if they can find stable, moist sand above the high-tide mark. If the turtles hatch, they can be confused by all the lights around them and may crawl toward the brightness of a resort or highway instead of the sea.

There used to be millions of sea turtles, and now there are only several thousand. However, by working to protect nesting sites, provide safe care for the eggs, and establish new nesting beaches, people hope to dramatically increase the number of turtles in the sea.